ELEVAITH
Trusting God, Growing Spiritually

DAILY DEVOTIONAL

ELVY MCLAURIN

Copyright © 2025 by Elvy McLaurin
All rights reserved.

Greatness Discovered Publishing
New Orleans, LA 70112
Phone: 504-556-2234
www.greatnessdiscoveredpublishing.com

All rights reserved. No part of this publication may be reproduced, stored in a retrieval system, or transmitted in any form or by any means-electronic, mechanical, digital, photocopy, recording, or any other except for brief quotations in printed reviews, without the prior permission of the author.

Text design and Book Cover Design by Charlyn Samson

All scripture quotations, unless otherwise indicated,
are taken from The Holy Bible.

ISBN: 979-8-9997613-0-9 (paperback)

CONTENTS

Foreword v
Opening Prayer vii
Acknowledgements..ix
Introduction...xi
How to Journey Through This Devotional xiii

Day 1:   Listen in Stillness 1
Day 2:   Speak with God First 8
Day 3:   From Tragedy to Triumph 15
Day 4:   In Due Time 23
Day 5:   Leave the Past Behind 31
Day 6:   Fearfully and Wonderfully Made..........................39
Day 7:   Affirmed by God...47
Day 8:   Molded Through Adversity 55
Day 9:   Strength in Silence 63
Day 10: Aligned with His Will 71
Day 11: Endure the Test 79
Day 12: Blessed and Highly Favored 87
Day 13: Forgive and Be Blessed 95
Day 14: Prepared for Greater..103
Day 15: Greater Suffering, Greater Glory 111
Day 16: Please God Over People 119
Day 17: Joy Despite Disappointment 127
Day 18: The Lord Is My Portion 135
Day 19: Trust God's Leading 143
Day 20: Ambition and Contentment 151
Day 21: New Birth Beyond Affliction 159
Day 22: Feelings Aren't Facts..167

Day 23: Positioned for Purpose 175
Day 24: Your Season of Favor 183
Day 25: Known by Your Fruit 191
Day 26: Salt and Light 199
Day 27: Obedience Over Perfection 207
Day 28: Divine Alignment 215
Day 29: Trust the Blueprint..222
Day 30: Strengthen Your Faith 230

Congratulations!...237
Scripture References for Trusting God in Times of Uncertainty..239
Scripture References for Spiritual Growth and Maturity............241
Scripture References for God's Faithfulness..................................243
Scripture References for Walking by Faith 245
Scripture References for Surrender and Obedience 247
Scripture References for Strength in Trials 249

About the Author..251

FOREWORD

Hey there,

I'm so glad you're holding this devotional by Elvy McLaurin! If your days ever feel overwhelming(and let's be real—they do), carving out just a few minutes to read Scripture, pray, reflect, and jot down your heart is like a shot of hope and joy straight to the soul.

Inside, you'll find bite-sized, Bible-based reflections and plenty of room for your own prayers and thoughts. There's something powerful in watching your own words spill onto the page—it turns your inner whispers into a genuine heart-to-heart with God and equips you to live out that faith boldly.

My prayer is simple: may this devotional be your daily refuge—a place where God's voice cuts through the noise, where you find clarity, courage, and fresh joy. Remember, you're never alone; you're fully seen, deeply loved, and your story matters.

Enjoy the journey, and I can't wait to hear how God surprises you with grace and peace through these pages (and your pen).

With all my heart,
Karen Bryan-Chambers

OPENING PRAYER

Heavenly Father,

Thank You for the gift of this devotional and the opportunity to share Your word with others. You have called me, equipped me, and entrusted me to be a light for Your glory. May my light shine brightly before others, reflecting Your goodness and leading many to give glory to You, our Father in heaven.

Lord, I lift up every reader of this devotional to You. Open their hearts and minds to receive Your word with clarity, wisdom, and understanding. May they find peace in Your presence and purpose in Your promises.

I pray that each reader is intentional in spending time with You, aligning their steps with Your will. Renew their minds and refresh their spirits with a renewed zeal for life. May they embrace the transformation You have in store for them and boldly walk in the path You have set before them.

Thank You, Lord, for this moment, for this gift, and for choosing me to share Your truth. May all who read these words be blessed and empowered to live out their God-given purpose.

In Jesus' mighty name,
Amen.

ACKNOWLEDGEMENTS

First and foremost, thank you, God. You knew me before I was formed in my mother's womb. You've always known who I am, whose I am, and who I'd become. I give You all honor, glory, and praise for the work You have done and are doing in my life. Thank You for using me as a vessel for Your word, allowing me to be a beacon of light to those I encounter.

To my family, friends, and supporters—thank you for your prayers, encouragement, and unwavering belief in my mission. Your love and support inspires me to keep moving forward.

To every reader of this devotional, thank you for taking this journey of faith with me. My prayer is that these pages provide guidance, comfort, and hope as you deepen your relationship with God.

INTRODUCTION

Elevatih: *The act of confident trust and the development of spiritual maturity.*

Welcome to *"Elevaith: Trusting God, Growing Spiritually,"*

You may be asking yourself what is "Spiritual Maturity" or am I there yet?

Spiritual maturity is learning to trust God even when you don't understand. It helps you to choose faith over fear, peace over panic, and prayer over control. This includes surrendering to His will over leading with what we have planned.

It better prepares you to respond under pressure instead of reacting. It allows you to show compassion to yourself and others. It reminds you to turn back to God even when you fall.

It's giving you the confidence to live what you believe, giving grace to yourself and others along the way, and letting every season—especially the hard ones, grow you deeper in faith.

This devotional is designed to nurture a deeper connection with God, inspire meaningful growth, and foster a mindset grounded in unwavering faith. My name is Elvy McLaurin, and it is my honor to walk with you on this transformative journey.

Every step toward God is a step closer to becoming the best version of yourself. Through these daily devotionals, we'll explore how to listen for God's voice, embrace His wisdom, and allow the Holy Spirit to influence our decisions, relationships, and purpose.

This book isn't just about reading—it's about living. Each reflection is an invitation to pause, meditate, and align your heart with God's will. It's about taking intentional steps toward spiritual maturity while learning to trust in God's timing and plans.

I want to encourage you to approach this journey with openness and intention. Pray, reflect, and take action as you feel led. Remember, spiritual maturity is not a destination but a continual process of growth. Together, let's embrace *Elevaith*, a confident trust in God and a commitment to developing spiritual sustainability.

Let's embark on this journey of transformation together.

In His Service,
Elvy McLaurin
Founder & CEO, Elevaith

HOW TO JOURNEY THROUGH THIS DEVOTIONAL

Each day on this journey, you will find:

1. **Opening Scripture**: A verse to meditate on.
2. **Daily Reflection**: A faith-based lesson or thought for the day.
3. **Prayer:** A written prayer to guide your conversation with God.
4. **Application**: A simple task to help you apply the lesson and foster spiritual growth.
5. **Contemplation**: A calm, meditative space to journal your reflections, thoughts, feelings, "aha" moments, and gratitude.

There's no right or wrong way to respond—just write from the heart. These pages are for your thoughts, your growth, and your connection with God. Let your words flow from wherever you feel led.

Although *Elevaith: Trusting God, Growing Spiritually* is structured as a 30-day devotional, it's not meant to be read in order. Let the Holy Spirit guide you. You might begin at the end, jump into the middle, or return to a day you've already read. Trust that you'll be led to the chapter your spirit needs in that moment.

For example, your "Day 1" might actually begin with what's labeled Day 6. That's perfectly okay. This devotional was designed with flexibility and freedom in mind. You'll also find 2 pages of journaling space—enough to revisit and reflect on each devotional monthly throughout the year.

What spoke to you in one season may speak to you differently in another. Day 6 in January may take on a deeper, richer meaning in July, shaped by your growth, experiences, and spiritual maturity. This was **intentional.** I designed this devotional so you can revisit, relearn, and respond from wherever you are in your faith journey.

DAY 1

Listen in Stillness

Opening Scripture:

"Be still, and know that I am God." – Psalm 46:10(a) (NKJV)

Daily Reflection:

Thinking you are right doesn't make it right. When faced with decisions or uncertainty, it's easy to rely on your own understanding. But as believers, we are called to seek God's wisdom above all else. Take time today to consult with God. Sit in His presence, and let the Holy Spirit lead you.

God often speaks in the stillness—those quiet, consecrated moments where your heart is open, and distractions fade. His voice might not come as a thunderous command but as a soft whisper in your spirit. Remember, the softer He speaks, the louder you will hear Him if you are truly listening.

Prayer:

Heavenly Father, teach me to be still in Your presence. Help me quiet my mind and heart to hear Your voice clearly. Lead me with Your wisdom, Holy Spirit, and guide my steps according to Your will. In Jesus' name, Amen.

Application:

Spend 10 minutes in silence today. Turn off all distractions—your phone, TV, and even music. Sit in a quiet place, close your eyes, and ask God to speak to your heart.

Contemplation:

- How did I feel sitting in God's presence?

_____

_____

_____

_____

_____

- What did I hear in the stillness today?

_____

_____

_____

_____

_____

_____

DAY 2

Speak with God First

Opening Scripture:

"If any of you lacks wisdom, you should ask God, who gives generously to all without finding fault, and it will be given to you." – James 1:5 (NIV)

Daily Reflection:

Before you confront someone or approach a difficult conversation, go to God first. Ask Him to prepare your heart and the other person's heart to receive. Seek His guidance for your words so they are wise, kind, and aligned with His will.

It's not enough to be right in your intentions—you must be Christ-like in your delivery. God has the power to soften hearts, open minds, and align your words with His purpose. Trust Him to make a way where there seems to be no way and bring peace to every situation.

Prayer:

Lord, before I speak, help me consult with You first. Guide my words with kindness, wisdom, and truth. Prepare the hearts of those I speak to, giving them ears to listen and minds to understand. Let my words bring healing and reflect Your love. In Jesus' name, Amen.

Application:

Think of a conversation you've been avoiding or a person you've been hesitant to confront. Take 5 minutes to pray specifically for wisdom, courage, and for God to prepare the other person's heart. Write out what you feel God is guiding you to say.

Contemplation:

- What is God teaching me about communication today?

_____
_____
_____
_____
_____

- How can I approach difficult conversations with love and wisdom?

_____
_____
_____
_____
_____

DAY 3

From Tragedy to Triumph

Opening Scripture:

"And we know that in all things God works for the good of those who love him, who have been called according to his purpose." – Romans 8:28 (NIV)

Daily Reflection:

Life's challenges can feel overwhelming, and at times, the pain of your current situation might make it difficult to see a way forward. But remember, God is the ultimate storyteller. He takes what was meant for harm and transforms it into something glorious. The moments that seem like setbacks are often setups for something greater.

You may not understand why things are happening the way they are, but trust that God is connecting the dots. The picture God is painting is bigger than what you can see right now. Believe in His promises, and know that everything is working together for your good and His glory.

What feels like a tragedy today can be your testimony tomorrow—a triumphant story of His faithfulness. Let go of the need to understand every detail and rest in the truth that God has a plan, and His timing is perfect.

Prayer:

Lord, thank You for working all things together for my good and for Your glory. Help me to trust You when life feels uncertain or painful. Give me the strength to walk by faith, not by sight, and to believe in the beautiful destiny You have for me. Turn my trials into triumphs, and let my life be a testimony of Your goodness. In Jesus' name, Amen.

Application:

Take 5 minutes today to reflect on a past difficulty that God turned into a blessing. Write it down as a reminder of His faithfulness. Pray and surrender it to God, trusting that he will work it out for your good.

Contemplation:

- What situation am I struggling to see from God's perspective (the bigger picture) that I can surrender to Him today?

_____

_____

_____

_____

_____

- How do I keep my faith strong while waiting for God's plan to unfold?

_____

_____

_____

_____

_____

_____

DAY 4

In Due Time

Opening Scripture:

"Let us not become weary in doing good, for at the proper time we will reap a harvest if we do not give up." – Galatians 6:9 (NIV)

Daily Reflection:

In a world that glorifies speed and instant gratification, feeling rushed can rob you of peace and perspective. When you feel the pressure to move quickly—whether in conversations, decisions, or tasks—pause and remind yourself: **in due time**. God's timing is never late, never early, but always perfect.

When you're tempted to speak hastily or act out of impatience, ask God to guide your words, slow your spirit, and help you to listen before speaking. Sometimes, the best thing you can do is sit with it, wait, and let God's wisdom guide your next step.

God has placed a "due time" calling over your life. There are seasons for sowing, growing, watering, and harvesting. Trust the process and seek His instructions daily. Ask Him to remind you of past steps He's called you to take and give you the strength to carry them out today. When you reap the harvest, let your first act be to give Him glory—for He is good, and His faithfulness endures forever.

Patience is more than waiting; it's about trusting God's process with joy, hope, and faithfulness. As Romans 12:12 says, "Be joyful in hope, patient in affliction, and faithful in prayer."

Prayer:

Heavenly Father, when I feel rushed, remind me of Your perfect timing. Help me to be quick to listen, slow to speak, and even slower to act without Your guidance. Strengthen my faith to wait for Your due time, and guide me to carry out the steps You've placed before me today. Let my life and my harvest bring glory to Your name. In Jesus' name, Amen.

Application:

Take a moment today to reflect on something you feel rushed about—whether it's a decision, a conversation, or a goal. Surrender it to God in prayer. Then, commit to waiting patiently for His timing.

Contemplation:

- How can I glorify God in the waiting and in the harvest?

  _____
  _____
  _____
  _____
  _____

- What instruction has God given me in the past that I can apply as a reminder?

  _____
  _____
  _____
  _____
  _____
  _____

DAY 5

Leave the Past Behind

Opening Scripture:

"Forget the former things; do not dwell on the past. See, I am doing a new thing! Now it springs up; do you not perceive it?" – Isaiah 43:18-19 (a) (NIV)

Daily Reflection:

The past has a way of lingering—affecting how you think, feel, and act in the present. Whether it's pain, regret, guilt, or even nostalgia, if the past is still influencing you, it's not truly behind you. God is calling you to let go of the past, so you can fully embrace the new thing He's doing in your life.

Holding on to what's behind you prevents you from walking forward into the destiny God has prepared for you. You don't have to ignore the lessons you've learned, but don't allow the wounds to define you. Release the grip of old pain and outdated narratives. Surrender them to God, and trust Him to bring healing, restoration, and purpose.

Ask yourself today: Is the past still present in my heart and mind? If the answer is yes, take it to God in prayer. The cross of Christ is a place of exchange—your burdens for His peace, your pain for His joy, your brokenness for His wholeness. He's doing a new thing. Let Him.

Prayer:

Heavenly Father, thank You for being the God of new beginnings. I release the past to You today. Heal the wounds I still carry, and renew my heart and mind. Help me to stop dwelling on what's behind me and focus on the future You have promised me. Show me how to walk forward in faith, leaving behind the things that no longer serve Your purpose for my life. In Jesus' name, Amen.

Application:

Take a quiet moment to write down anything from your past that is still affecting you today—whether it's a hurt, a mistake, or an unresolved situation.

Contemplation:

- What from my past is still present in my life today?

  _____
  _____
  _____
  _____

- How is God asking me to release it?

  _____
  _____
  _____
  _____

- What steps can I take to leave the past behind and embrace His new plan for me?

  _____
  _____
  _____
  _____

DAY 6

Fearfully and Wonderfully Made

Opening Scripture:

"I will praise You, for I am fearfully and wonderfully made; Marvelous are Your works, And that my soul knows very well." – Psalm 139:14 (NKJV)

Daily Reflection:

You are God's masterpiece, intentionally crafted with love and purpose. How often do we let the opinions of others or our own insecurities diminish the beauty of who we are? It's time to celebrate yourself and love yourself as God loves you.

God didn't make a mistake when He created you. Every part of you—your personality, your strengths, your quirks, and even your flaws—is part of His divine design. He knew you before you were formed in your mother's womb, and He calls you **fearfully and wonderfully made**.

Do not dislike yourself because someone else cannot see your value. Remember, you were made to glorify God, not to conform to the world's expectations. Free yourself from comparison, the need to please others, and the pressure to be someone you are not. Instead, live fully, abundantly, and unapologetically as the person God created you to be.

When you love yourself and find peace within, you reflect the love of the Creator who formed you in His image. Celebrate the unique person that you are, and live each day knowing that God so loved you, He gave His only Son so that you might have life—and have it abundantly.

Prayer:

Lord, thank You for creating me fearfully and wonderfully. Help me to see myself through Your eyes and love myself as You love me. Free me from the chains of comparison and the desire to please others. Teach me to celebrate the person You have made me to be and to live with boldness, joy, and peace. In Jesus' name, Amen.

Application:

Take some time today to celebrate yourself. Write down five things you love about yourself—traits, talents, or qualities that make you unique. If you struggle to think of them, ask God to reveal how He sees you. Place this list somewhere visible as a daily reminder of your worth.

Contemplation:

- How can I live more unapologetically as the person God created me to be?

_____
_____
_____
_____
_____
_____

- What areas of my life need freedom from comparison or people-pleasing?

_____
_____
_____
_____
_____
_____

DAY 7

Affirmed by God

Opening Scripture:

"Greater love has no one than this, than to lay down one's life for his friends." – John 15:13 (NKJV)

Daily Reflection:

Your worth is not determined by the opinions of others, but by the immeasurable love of God. Jesus Christ gave His life for you—not because of what you've achieved, what you look like, or how others see you, but because He loves you unconditionally. His willingness to die for you is the ultimate affirmation of your value.

It's easy to fall into the trap of seeking validation from people, measuring yourself by their approval or criticism. But human opinions are fleeting, imperfect, and often flawed. God's love, however, is eternal and unchanging. Your worth was settled the moment Jesus stretched out His arms on the cross and declared, "It is finished."

When you anchor your worth in the love of God, you free yourself from the exhausting pursuit of people-pleasing. Rest in the truth that you are already accepted, cherished, and loved by the One who matters most. Let this truth guide your thoughts, actions, and relationships.

Prayer:

Lord, thank You for affirming my worth through Your sacrifice. Help me to stop seeking validation from others and to rest in the truth of Your love. Teach me to value myself as You value me and to live boldly, knowing that my worth is found in You alone. In Jesus' name, Amen.

Application:

Reflect on areas in your life where you've sought the approval of others. Write them down and release them to God in prayer.

Contemplation:

- How does John 15:13 remind me of my worth?

  _____
  _____
  _____
  _____
  _____
  _____

- What are some declarations that affirm my worth and can be spoken over myself daily? (e.g., "I am loved, chosen, and worthy because of Christ")

  _____
  _____
  _____
  _____
  _____
  _____

DAY 8

Molded Through Adversity

Opening Scripture:

"No weapon formed against you shall prosper, and every tongue which rises against you in judgment you shall condemn. This is the heritage of the servants of the Lord, and their righteousness is from Me," says the Lord." – Isaiah 54:17 (NKJV)

Daily Reflection:

Adversity is not your downfall—it's your opportunity. Every trial you face has the potential to mold you into the person God created you to be. In the face of difficulty, declare: **No weapon formed against me shall prosper.**

Discomfort often feels unbearable, but it is in these moments of stretching and refining that God shapes your character. Like clay in the hands of the potter, He is molding you for a purpose greater than you can imagine. Trust His hands, even when the process feels painful.

Pray for the pruning of anything in your life that doesn't align with God's will. It may hurt to let go, but know that God is creating a stronger, healthier, and more fruitful version of you. Your trials are not meaningless—they are building your resilience, endurance, and faith.

When your heart feels weary, hold on to God's promises. Even faith as small as a mustard seed is enough to move mountains. Remind yourself daily that the enemy cannot have your mind, body, or soul because you belong to the Lord. Trust Him to work through every hardship, knowing that your trials today will become your testimony tomorrow.

Prayer:

Lord, I trust You as the potter and surrender myself as clay. Mold me into the person You've called me to be. Trim away anything in my life that is not of You, and strengthen my heart in the face of adversity. Help me to hold on to my faith, even when it feels small, and remind me that my trials are working together for my good and Your glory. In Jesus' name, Amen.

Application:

Take a moment today to reflect on your current trials. Write down how you believe these challenges could strengthen your character or draw you closer to God. Then, speak Isaiah 54:17 over your life, declaring that no weapon formed against you shall prosper.

Contemplation:

- What branches or vines in my life need to be trimmed away?

_____
_____
_____
_____
_____

- How can I hold firm to God's promises, even when I feel weary?

_____
_____
_____
_____
_____

DAY 9

Strength in Silence

Opening Scripture:

"For this is the will of God, that by doing good you may put to silence the ignorance of foolish men." – 1 Peter 2:15 (NKJV)

Daily Reflection:

Sometimes, the greatest act of faith is staying silent. When emotions rise and words are ready to pour out, God calls us to pause, to trust, and to let Him take control. Silence is not weakness; it's strength. It's surrendering your need to be heard or understood to the One who knows all and sees all.

Consider the Israelites marching around Jericho. They remained silent for six days, obeying God's command, even though they likely didn't fully understand His plan. Their silence wasn't inactivity—it was trust in action. And on the seventh day, their faith unleashed God's power, and the walls came tumbling down.

When lies are spoken about you or you feel misunderstood, remember this: staying silent doesn't mean you agree or that the truth doesn't matter. It means you trust that God's will is greater than your need to defend yourself. Your silence is a declaration of faith that He is working behind the scenes for your good and His glory.

There is strength in silence because silence makes room for God's miracles. In your quietness, His power is made perfect. Trust Him to fight your battles, to bring clarity, and to vindicate you in His time.

Prayer:

Lord, teach me to be silent when You call me to be. Help me to trust that You are working all things together for my good, even when I feel misunderstood or falsely accused. Guard my heart and my tongue, and remind me that Your will is more important than my need to be heard. Thank You for being my defender and for the lessons You teach me in the stillness. In Jesus' name, Amen.

Application:

Reflect on moments when you've spoken out of anger or frustration. Think about how those situations might have been different if you had chosen silence. The next time you feel the urge to speak impulsively, pause and pray for guidance. Ask God for the strength to hold your peace and trust Him with the outcome.

Contemplation:

- What situations in my life are calling for silence and trust?

  _____

  _____

  _____

  _____

  _____

- When has my silence allowed God to work in ways I didn't expect?

  _____

  _____

  _____

  _____

  _____

  _____

DAY 10

Aligned with His Will

Opening Scripture:

"The steps of a good man are ordered by the Lord, and He delights in his way. Though he fall, he shall not be utterly cast down; for the Lord upholds him with His hand." – Psalm 37:23-24 (NKJV)

Daily Reflection:

When we are out of line, we are not aligned. Alignment with God's will and His word is key to walking in purpose and peace. The good news is that when we stray or fall short, God's grace is abundant. He is not waiting to condemn us—He is waiting to restore us.

Feeling remorse for being out of line is a sign of a heart that seeks God. It shows integrity, self-awareness, and the desire to grow. Celebrate that trait within yourself, and let it motivate you to do better. Each day is an opportunity to step closer to alignment with God's will.

Remember, your personal journey is not a race or a competition. The only person you're trying to be better than is who **you** were yesterday. Stop beating yourself up for past mistakes and give yourself grace. God's love is bigger than your failures, and His forgiveness is greater than your guilt.

God doesn't judge you as harshly as you judge yourself. He sees your effort, your heart, and your desire to align with Him. Show yourself compassion, knowing that His mercies are new every morning. You are loved by Him and worthy of kindness—not just from others, but from yourself.

Prayer:

Lord, thank You for Your grace and mercy. Forgive me when I fall short, and help me to realign with Your will for my life. Teach me to be kind and compassionate toward myself as You are with me. Strengthen my heart to grow closer to You each day and to let go of self-condemnation. In Jesus' name, Amen.

Application:

Identify a situation in your life where you feel out of alignment with God's will. Write it down and ask for His forgiveness. Then, write a plan for how you can do better moving forward.

Contemplation:

- What area of my life needs realignment with God's will?

  _____
  _____
  _____
  _____

- What steps can I take to grow closer to God and realign my life with His will?

  _____
  _____
  _____
  _____

- How can I show myself more compassion and grace today?

  _____
  _____
  _____
  _____

DAY 11

Endure the Test

Opening Scripture:

"Behold, I will do a new thing, now it shall spring forth; shall you not know it? I will even make a road in the wilderness and rivers in the desert." – Isaiah 43:19 (NKJV)

Daily Reflection:

Without a test, there is no testimony. The challenges you face today are shaping you for the abundant life God has prepared for you. Endure it! Trust that God is moving you into a season of abundance, overflow, favor, and newness. He is doing a new thing in your life—can you see it?

To fully embrace what God has in store for you, you must let go of the former things that weigh you down. Leave behind old hurts, failures, and fears, and step forward with faith. Open your eyes to see His blessings, your ears to hear His voice, your mind to understand His plan, and your heart to obey.

Your best days are not behind you; they are ahead of you, closer than you think. Trust that God's timing is perfect, and praise Him in advance for what He's already working out on your behalf. The victory is already yours. Keep the faith and endurance, for your testimony will bring glory to His name and inspire others to trust Him too.

Prayer:

Lord, thank You for the tests that strengthen my faith and lead to my testimony. Help me to endure with patience and trust that You are working all things for my good. Open my eyes to see Your blessings, my ears to hear Your guidance, and my heart to embrace the new things You are doing in my life. I praise You in advance for the victory, overflow, and favor You are bringing. In Jesus' name, Amen.

Application:

Take a moment to reflect on past challenges that became testimonies of God's faithfulness. Write down how God brought you through them. Then, think about your current test and write a declaration of faith, thanking God for the victory that's already on the way.

Contemplation:

- What past challenges has God turned into testimonies of His faithfulness in my life?

_____
_____
_____
_____
_____
_____

- How did those experiences shape my trust in Him?

_____
_____
_____
_____
_____
_____

DAY 12

Blessed and Highly Favored

Opening Scripture:

"And the Lord was with Joseph, and he was a prosperous man; and he was in the house of his master the Egyptian." – Genesis 39:2 (KJV)

Daily Reflection:

I want to remind you today that the Lord is with you in all that you do. His favor surrounds you, and He will make everything you put your hands to, to prosper. Whether you're in the city or the field, your homes, your work, and your life are blessed. **You** are blessed and highly favored. Stand on that truth and give God the thanks, glory, honor, and praise He deserves!

God is faithful to His promises. He will do exactly what He said He would do. Even when the circumstances seem uncertain or the situation feels overwhelming, hold fast to His word with unwavering faith. His plan is greater than what you can see, and His power works beyond what you can comprehend.

Sometimes, before the rise comes betrayal, hardship, or testing. But don't let temporary challenges make you lose sight of the greatness God has in store for you. You are on the rise to your God-ordained purpose. Believe it in your heart, feel it in your spirit, and embody it in your actions. This is how you step into the abundant blessings and favor He has already prepared for you.

Remember, you are standing on your Father's business, and **He** has the final say— not man. Trust Him, for His favor is greater than any opposition.

Prayer:

Father, thank You for Your presence in my life and for Your favor that surrounds me. I stand on Your promises, knowing that You will do what You said You would do. Help me to trust You even in uncertain times and to walk boldly in the blessings You have already declared over my life. I give You all the glory, honor, and praise. In Jesus' name, Amen.

Application:

Take a moment to list the areas in your life where you've seen God's favor. Speak aloud words of gratitude for each one. Then, declare God's promises over the areas where you are still waiting for breakthrough, trusting that He will bring them to pass.

Contemplation:

- How can I embody the mindset of being blessed and highly favored in my daily action?

_____

_____

_____

_____

_____

- How can I embrace the new things God is doing in my life?

_____

_____

_____

_____

_____

DAY 13

Forgive and Be Blessed

Opening Scripture:

"A thousand may fall at your side, ten thousand at your right hand, but it will not come near you." – Psalm 91:7 (NKJV)

Daily Reflection:

There will be times when people speak harshly about you or judge you, unaware of the silent battles you're already facing—or perhaps aware but lacking compassion. Despite this, remember that God sees your heart and your pain, and He will bless you abundantly because of your endurance and faith. The greater the problem, the greater the blessing waiting for you on the other side.

Do not let the words or actions of others harden your heart. Instead, adopt a heart posture of forgiveness. Those who spoke ill of you or mistreated you may know what they did, but they often don't understand the depth of how it affected you. Even still, our Father teaches us to forgive, just as Jesus said on the cross: *"Forgive them, for they know not what they do."*

Leave vengeance to the Lord. He is your vindicator and defender. Trust that He will make all things right in His timing. No matter what trials you face, God will bring you through the fire without a trace of smoke. He is your protector, your shield, and your deliverer. Stand firm in the promise that greater is He who is in you than he who is in the world.

Prayer:

Father, thank You for being my vindicator and my shield. Help me to forgive those who have hurt me, whether intentionally or unintentionally. Teach me to release bitterness and adopt a heart posture of grace and compassion. I trust You to handle every situation and to bless me abundantly in Your perfect timing. In Jesus' name, Amen.

Application:

Think of someone who has hurt or wronged you. Take a moment to forgive them in prayer, asking God to heal your heart and theirs. Then, release the situation into God's hands, trusting Him to vindicate you and bless you in due time.

Contemplation:

- Who do I need to forgive today, and what steps can I take to release the hurt to God?

  _____
  _____
  _____
  _____

- How have I seen God protect and vindicate me in the past?

  _____
  _____
  _____
  _____

- What blessings am I believing for as I endure this season with faith and grace?

  _____
  _____
  _____
  _____

DAY 14

Prepared for Greater

Opening Scripture:

"Blessed is the one who perseveres under trial because, having stood the test, that person will receive the crown of life that the Lord has promised to those who love him." – James 1:12 (NIV)

Daily Reflection:

If God didn't allow you to experience trials, you wouldn't know how to war in the Spirit. Every challenge, every battle, and every difficulty is meant to shape you into who God has called you to be. He is preparing you for greater—greater blessings, greater responsibility, and greater purpose.

In this preparation, God is developing your character so that you can steward His blessings properly. He wants you to have wisdom, knowledge, and understanding, all of which are refined through the tests and trials you endure. These moments are not meant to break you but to strengthen you, equipping you for the promises He has spoken over your life.

Trust the process. Though it may be hard to see in the moment, every experience—both good and bad—is part of His divine plan for your life. Lean into Him, seek His guidance, and allow Him to equip you with the tools you need for the next level of your journey.

Prayer:

Lord, thank You for every trial and challenge that has strengthened my faith and built my character. Help me to see Your hand in every situation, knowing You are preparing me for greater. Give me wisdom, understanding, and the ability to steward Your blessings well. In Jesus' name, Amen.

Application:

Take time to reflect on a past trial or challenge that helped you grow spiritually, mentally, or emotionally. Write down how God used that experience to develop your character. Then, pray for the strength and wisdom to face your current challenges with faith and perseverance.

Contemplation:

- How is God using my current circumstances to develop my character?

- What areas of my life do I need to surrender to Him to gain wisdom and understanding?

DAY 15

Greater Suffering, Greater Glory

Opening Scripture:

"For I consider that the sufferings of this present time are not worthy to be compared with the glory which shall be revealed in us." – Romans 8:18 (NKJV)

Daily Reflection:

The more you endure suffering, the greater your testimony and the greater the blessing that follows. Your life is a living testimony of God's grace and faithfulness. Every trial, every tear, every moment of hardship is an opportunity for God to show His power, His provision, and His unwavering presence in your life.

Remember, God is with you every step of the way. Even when it feels like you're walking through the fire, He is refining you, shaping you, and carrying you through to your breakthrough. When you come out on the other side, your story will be a reflection of His goodness and mercy, a light for others to see that He was with you all along.

Let your life be a testimony that gives God the glory. When people look at your life and see the victory He has given you, they will know that it was only by His grace and favor. Your suffering will not be in vain—it will be the foundation for a testimony that touches hearts, changes lives, and glorifies the Lord.

Prayer:

Lord, thank You for turning my suffering into a testimony that reflects Your grace and glory. Help me to endure with faith, knowing that my struggles are not in vain. Use my life as a living example of

Your goodness, that others may see You through me. In Jesus' name, Amen.

Application:

Take a moment to reflect on a time in your life when God turned your pain into a blessing. Share that testimony with someone today who may need encouragement, reminding them that God is with them just as He was with you.

Contemplation:

- What current challenges can I trust Him to turn into a testimony?

_____
_____
_____
_____
_____
_____

- How can I use my testimony to encourage and inspire others?

_____
_____
_____
_____
_____
_____

DAY 16

Please God Over People

Opening Scripture:

"Am I now trying to win the approval of human beings, or of God? Or am I trying to please people? If I were still trying to please people, I would not be a servant of Christ." – Galatians 1:10 (NIV)

Daily Reflection:

Pleasing others in a healthy and balanced way—while maintaining your self-respect—is an act of kindness and love. However, people-pleasing at the expense of your values, boundaries, or well-being can compromise your integrity and spiritual walk. The distinction lies in your intention: Are you seeking to honor God, or are you seeking approval from others?

You may not always like what you have to do, but as long as your actions align with God's Word and His will, you can be confident that you're on the right path. Pleasing God often requires courage, sacrifice, and standing firm in your beliefs, even if it makes others uncomfortable.

Remember, your ultimate goal is to glorify God, not to satisfy the fleeting opinions of others. God sees your heart, your effort, and your obedience. Keep Him at the center of your decisions, and He will reward your faithfulness. Seek to please God, and the right relationships and opportunities will follow.

Prayer:

Lord, help me to focus on pleasing You above all else. Teach me how to maintain healthy relationships without compromising my self-respect or my values. Give me the courage to do the right thing, even when it's difficult. Let my actions always honor You. In Jesus' name, Amen.

Application:

Examine a recent decision or situation where you felt pressured to compromise your values to please others. Reflect on how you can handle similar situations in the future by prioritizing God's will over human approval.

Contemplation:

- In what ways have I been compromising myself to please others?

  _____
  _____
  _____
  _____

- How can I set healthy boundaries while maintaining kindness and respect?

  _____
  _____
  _____
  _____

- What specific steps can I take to focus on pleasing God instead of seeking validation from others?

  _____
  _____
  _____
  _____

DAY 17

Joy Despite Disappointment

Opening Scripture:

*Then he said to them, "Go your way, eat the fat, drink the sweet, and send portions to those for whom nothing is prepared; for this day is holy to our Lord. Do not sorrow, for the joy of the L*ORD *is your strength—* Nehemiah 8:10 (NKJV)

Daily Reflection:

Disappointment is an inevitable part of life. Plans may fall apart, people may let you down, and circumstances may not unfold as expected. But even in the face of disappointment, you have the power to hold on to your joy. Your joy is your responsibility, and it is not tied to external outcomes or temporary situations—it is rooted in God.

The joy of the Lord is unshakable and ever-present. It sustains you through life's difficulties and gives you the strength to press forward when things don't go your way. Joy isn't the absence of problems but the presence of God in your life.

When disappointment strikes, lean into His Word, His promises, and His presence. Choose to focus on His goodness and the blessings that remain. Let gratitude and faith be your response. Joy is not something the world can give or take away—it's your inheritance as a child of God. Guard it, nurture it, and let it shine, even in the darkest moments.

Prayer:

Lord, thank You for being the source of my joy, even when life doesn't go as planned. Help me to guard my joy and not let disappointment steal it away. Strengthen my faith and remind me that Your plans are greater than my own. In Jesus' name, Amen.

Application:

When disappointment arises today, take a moment to pause, breathe, and reflect on three things you're grateful for. Write them down as a reminder that God's blessings and joy are still present in your life.

Contemplation:

- What recent disappointment have I allowed to affect my joy?

  _____

  _____

  _____

  _____

  _____

  _____

- How can I shift my perspective and trust God's plan in this situation?

  _____

  _____

  _____

  _____

  _____

  _____

DAY 18

The Lord Is My Portion

Opening Scripture:

"The Lord is my portion," says my soul, "therefore I hope in Him." – Lamentations 3:24 (NKJV)

Daily Reflection:

The Lord Himself is our portion, our inheritance, and our everything. He is the source of every blessing, the foundation of our security, the provider of all our needs, and the anchor of our hope. When the world feels uncertain, when material possessions fade, or when people let us down, we can rest assured that the Lord remains constant and unchanging.

Recognizing God as our portion means that He alone is enough. He fills every void, meets every need, and satisfies every longing. When you depend on Him, you find that His provision is perfect, His protection is unfailing, and His love is boundless.

When you feel tempted to seek fulfillment from external things—be it success, approval, or material possessions—remember that true contentment comes from knowing that God is your ultimate source. As long as you have Him, you have everything you need.

Prayer:

Lord, thank You for being my portion and my source of everything good. Help me to rely on You fully and trust that You are enough for me. Teach me to see Your blessings in every moment and to place my hope in You alone. In Jesus' name, Amen.

Application:

Take a moment today to reflect on ways God has been your portion in the past. Write down specific instances where He has provided, protected, or sustained you. Let these reminders strengthen your faith in His unfailing nature.

Contemplation:

- Trusting that God is my source, what areas of my life do I need to surrender to Him?

  _____
  _____
  _____
  _____
  _____

- How can I deepen my relationship with the Lord to rely on Him more fully?

  _____
  _____
  _____
  _____
  _____

DAY 19

Trust God's Leading

Opening Scripture:

"Trust in the Lord with all your heart and lean not on your own understanding; in all your ways submit to Him, and He will make your paths straight." – Proverbs 3:5-6 (NIV)

Daily Reflection:

Obeying God requires faith, courage, and trust, even when you don't understand where He's leading you. God's ways are higher than our ways, and His plans are greater than we can imagine. Often, He calls us to step out in faith without revealing the full picture. It is in these moments of uncertainty that our trust in Him is tested and strengthened.

Faith is not about having all the answers—it's about trusting the One who does. Following God blindly is not an act of ignorance; it's an act of obedience and surrender. When you declare, "Lord, I trust You," you're inviting Him to take the lead and guide you into His divine purpose for your life.

You may not see the destination, but you can trust the One who holds the map. Trust that His plans are good, His timing is perfect, and His path will lead to blessings and growth beyond what you can comprehend.

Prayer:

Lord, I trust You. Even when I don't understand where You're leading me, I will obey Your call. Strengthen my faith and help me to walk in obedience with a heart full of trust and expectation. In Jesus' name, Amen.

Application:

Reflect on one thing God may be calling you to do, but fear or uncertainty has held you back. Take one actionable step toward it, declaring aloud, "Lord, I trust You."

Contemplation:

- How can I activate my faith and trust Him more deeply?

  _____
  _____
  _____
  _____
  _____

- What steps can I take today to walk boldly into His plan for me?

  _____
  _____
  _____
  _____
  _____
  _____

DAY 20

Ambition and Contentment

Opening Scripture:

"Not that I am speaking of being in need, for I have learned in whatever situation I am to be content. I know how to be brought low, and I know how to abound. In any and every circumstance, I have learned the secret of facing plenty and hunger, abundance and need. I can do all things through him who strengthens me." – Philippians 4:11-13 (ESV)

Daily Reflection:

Contentment does not mean complacency, and being satisfied with your present doesn't equate to settling for less than what you desire. Contentment is an acknowledgment of gratitude for what God has already done, even as you anticipate what He will do in the future. It's about trusting His timing and provision while still pursuing the vision He's placed on your heart.

An abundant mindset is rooted in the belief that God is able to provide all that you need and more. Scarcity is the belief that there is never enough, but abundance declares that with God, all things are possible. When you align yourself with an abundant mindset, you free yourself from the fear of lack and step into a life of faith, hope, and expectancy.

You can aspire for greatness and growth while maintaining a heart full of gratitude for where you are. The secret is understanding that joy, peace, and fulfillment are not tied to circumstances, but it's tied to your relationship with God. In Him, you find the strength to flourish in both seasons of plenty and seasons of need.

Prayer:

Lord, thank You for teaching me the value of contentment. Help me to remain grateful for where I am while trusting You to guide me toward the future You have for me. Give me the wisdom to balance gratitude with ambition and the courage to trust in Your abundant provision. In Jesus' name, Amen.

Application:

Reflect on one area of your life where you've been striving without gratitude. Write down three things you're thankful for in that area. Then, list one actionable step you can take to pursue your goals with faith in God's abundance.

Contemplation:

- What does contentment look like for me in this season of life?

  _____
  _____
  _____
  _____
  _____
  _____

- How can I shift my mindset from scarcity to abundance?

  _____
  _____
  _____
  _____
  _____
  _____

DAY 21

New Birth Beyond Affliction

Opening Scripture:

"For our light affliction, which is but for a moment, is working for us a far more exceeding and eternal weight of glory..." – 2 Corinthians 4:17 (NKJV)

Daily Reflection:

When you're in a place of affliction—whether physical, emotional, or spiritual—it can feel impossible to create, build, or birth something new. Affliction can weigh you down, cloud your vision, and sap your strength. But know this: God never intends for you to remain in that place. He has a plan to move you from pain to purpose, from affliction to abundance, and from struggle to strength.

Birthing requires a foundation of faith, hope, and trust in God's promises. Affliction, on the other hand, thrives on fear, doubt, and hopelessness. To step into the fullness of what God has called you to birth, you must allow Him to heal the wounds of affliction and replace them with His peace and strength.

Your affliction may be a season, but it is not your destiny. God wants to bring you to a place of restoration, where you can give birth to the dreams, visions, and blessings He has prepared for you. Trust in His timing and allow Him to transform your pain into purpose.

Prayer:

Lord, I release my affliction into Your hands and trust You to heal and restore me. Prepare me to birth the dreams You've placed in my heart.

Give me the strength and peace to move forward in faith, knowing that Your glory will be revealed in my life. In Jesus' name, Amen.

Application:

Identify the areas in your life where affliction is holding you back. Pray over those areas and ask God to begin the healing process. Take one small step today to move out of that place of affliction—whether it's journaling, seeking counsel, or dedicating time to worship and prayer.

Contemplation:

- What has God called me to birth, and how can I begin preparing for it?

_____
_____
_____
_____
_____
_____

- How can I invite God into my healing process?

_____
_____
_____
_____
_____
_____
_____

DAY 22

Feelings Aren't Facts

Opening Scripture:

"For my thoughts are not your thoughts, neither are your ways my ways," declares the Lord. "As the heavens are higher than the earth, so are my ways higher than your ways and my thoughts than your thoughts." – Isaiah 55:8-9 (NIV)

Daily Reflection:

Feelings are temporary and often influenced by our circumstances, but God's truth is eternal and unchanging. It's easy to let emotions dictate our actions or beliefs, but we must remind ourselves that feelings are not facts. Our feelings may tell us that we're not good enough, that things won't work out, or that God has forgotten us—but His Word reminds us that His plans for us are good, true, and faithful.

When you find yourself overwhelmed by emotions, take a moment to pause, pray, and reflect. Look back on the times God has come through for you in the past. Remind yourself of His promises and His faithfulness. Trust that even when your feelings tell you otherwise, God's plans are greater than what you can see or comprehend.

When doubt creeps in, choose to fill in the blanks with truth:

- *When I feel alone, I remind myself that God said, "I will never leave you nor forsake you."* (Hebrews 13:5(b))
- *When I feel unworthy, I remember that I am fearfully and wonderfully made.* (Psalm 139:14)
- *When I feel defeated, I stand on the promise that I can do all things through Christ who strengthens me.* (Philippians 4:13)

Prayer:

Lord, help me to remember that my feelings are not always reflective of Your truth. Teach me to stand on Your promises and not be swayed by emotions. Remind me of Your faithfulness and guide me in trusting Your plans for my life. In Jesus' name, Amen.

Application:

Write a list of God's promises in your journal. Then, reflect on specific times when He has fulfilled those promises in your life. Whenever your emotions feel overwhelming, refer back to this list as a reminder of His truth.

Contemplation:

- What emotions or feelings have been clouding my faith recently?

  _____
  _____
  _____
  _____
  _____

- How has God shown up for me in the past, even when I doubted?

  _____
  _____
  _____
  _____
  _____

DAY 23

Positioned for Purpose

Opening Scripture:

"But he said to me, 'My grace is sufficient for you, for my power is made perfect in weakness.' Therefore I will boast all the more gladly about my weaknesses, so that Christ's power may rest on me." – 2 Corinthians 12:9 (NIV)

Daily Reflection:

Sometimes, God has to remove you from your comfort zone to elevate you to new levels. Isolation isn't a punishment but a preparation. During this time, He refines you, shapes you, and opens your eyes to what and who truly serves His purpose for your life.

The challenging moments weren't for nothing—they were for your growth. They were necessary to give you wisdom, understanding, and discernment. God had to clear your path and reveal the truth, so you could walk boldly into His promises for your life.

You haven't even begun to scratch the surface of the blessings He has in store for you. The best is yet to come. Trust that every loss, disappointment, and trial was making room for better.

God is building a new community around you—people who honor and value you as you deserve. Embrace this transition with faith and gratitude, knowing that He is aligning your life with His divine purpose.

Prayer:

Lord, thank You for the seasons of isolation and elevation. Thank You for removing what doesn't serve me and for preparing me for what is ahead. Surround me with people who reflect Your love and light, and make me a vessel of Your goodness. Remove anything in me that is not of You and align my spirit with Your will. In Jesus' name, Amen.

Application:

Reflect on the people, habits, and situations God has removed from your life.

Write down qualities or values you desire in your new circle and season. Pray over this list and ask God to guide you to the right connections.

Contemplation:

- What moments of isolation have prepared me for elevation?

  _____
  _____
  _____
  _____

- How has God shown His grace during my weaknesses?

  _____
  _____
  _____
  _____

- What am I most looking forward to in this new season of my life?

  _____
  _____
  _____
  _____

DAY 24

Your Season of Favor

Opening Scripture:

"The Lord says to my lord: 'Sit at my right hand until I make your enemies a footstool for your feet.'" – Psalms 110:1 (NIV)

Daily Reflection:

Your time is coming, and the world will see God's hand upon your life. In moments when you feel overlooked, remember this: the last shall be first. God has been preparing you for your season of favor, and when it arrives, it will be undeniable.

There's no need for pride or bitterness—your blessings are not about revenge but about God's glory. He's using your life as a testimony of His faithfulness and favor. When people see the rapid overflow of blessings, your response should be simple and humble: *"It's all God."*

You're one of His favorites, cherished and chosen. Trust the process, knowing that He's aligning everything for your good and His glory. Keep walking in faith and obedience. Your "first" season is closer than you think.

Prayer:

Lord, thank You for reminding me that my time is coming. Help me to wait patiently, trust in Your perfect timing, and remain humble when my season of blessings arrives. May my life reflect Your goodness, and may I always give You the glory for the favor You've shown me. In Jesus' name, Amen.

Application:

Write down areas where you've felt "last" or overlooked. Reflect on how God has been working behind the scenes in those areas. Pray for the faith to trust in His timing and His promise to make you the head and not the tail.

Contemplation:

- How can I prepare my heart to receive His blessings with humility and gratitude?

_____
_____
_____
_____
_____

- What will I say to others about God's role in my blessings?

_____
_____
_____
_____
_____

DAY 25

Known by Your Fruit

Opening Scripture:

"But the fruit of the Spirit is love, joy, peace, forbearance, kindness, goodness, faithfulness, gentleness, and self-control. Against such things there is no law." – Galatians 5:22-23 (NIV)

Daily Reflection:

Our lives are a reflection of God's presence within us. The fruit of the Spirit isn't just a list of virtues; it's evidence of Christ dwelling in us. The way we love, the peace we carry, the kindness we show—all of it speaks louder than words.

When people encounter you, let them experience His love, His gentleness, His kindness. Your actions, words, and presence should point them back to the Lord Almighty. May your life be a beacon of His light, a testimony of His goodness, and a reminder of His grace.

We are called not just to speak about Christ but to live in such a way that others see Him in us. Ask yourself, "When others see me, do they see Him?" Let your fruit testify of the One who lives within you.

Prayer:

Lord, let my life bear the fruit of Your Spirit. May my love reflect Your love, my peace reflect Your peace, and my actions point others to You. Help me to walk daily in patience, kindness, and self-control, showing the world who You are through the way I live. In Jesus' name, Amen.

Application:

Take time today to reflect on the fruit of the Spirit. Which characteristics of the fruit are thriving in your life? Which ones need more attention and growth?

Contemplation:

- How can I better reflect God's love and peace in my actions and words?

  _____

  _____

  _____

  _____

- In what ways do I want people to experience Christ through me?

  _____

  _____

  _____

  _____

- What is one practical step that I can take to cultivate that fruit in my daily life?

  _____

  _____

  _____

  _____

DAY 26

Salt and Light

Opening Scripture:

"You are the salt of the earth. But if the salt loses its saltiness, how can it be made salty again? It is no longer good for anything, except to be thrown out and trampled underfoot. You are the light of the world. A town built on a hill cannot be hidden." – Matthew 5:13-14 (NIV)

Daily Reflection:

God created you to be a difference-maker. As the salt of the earth, you bring value, purpose, and preservation to a world in need of God's love and truth. Just as salt enhances the flavor of food, your presence enhances the lives of those around you by demonstrating the joy, hope, and love of Christ.

As the light of the world, you have the responsibility to illuminate the path to righteousness. In a world filled with darkness, your light is a beacon that points others toward God's grace and salvation. Your words, actions, and love should radiate His glory and truth.

Being salt and light means living intentionally. Ask yourself today: "Am I adding value to those around me? Am I shining brightly, even when the world tries to dim my light?"

Prayer:

Lord, thank You for calling me to be salt and light in this world. Help me to bring value, love, and truth into every situation. Let my light shine so brightly that others see You through me. Teach me to live in a way that glorifies You. In Jesus' name, Amen.

Application:

Be intentional about being a source of positivity and guidance today. Reflect on how your actions reflect God's love and truth.

Contemplation:

- How can I bring flavor and light into the lives of others today?

  _____
  _____
  _____
  _____

- In what areas of my life am I allowing my light to dim?

  _____
  _____
  _____
  _____

- How has God called me to be a source of guidance and hope for others?

  _____
  _____
  _____
  _____

DAY 27

Obedience Over Perfection

Opening Scripture:

"But He said to me, 'My grace is sufficient for you, for My power is made perfect in weakness.' Therefore I will boast all the more gladly about my weaknesses, so that Christ's power may rest on me." – 2 Corinthians 12:9 (NIV)

Daily Reflection:

God isn't looking for you to have it all together; He's looking for you to trust Him enough to take the first step. Perfection isn't the goal—obedience is. He doesn't call the qualified; He qualifies the called. The question isn't whether you're good enough, but whether you're willing to say, "Here I am, Lord, use me."

Submitting your will to God doesn't mean you lose your identity; it means aligning your desires with His divine plan. It's a declaration that you trust His ways more than your own. When you surrender, He can do exceedingly and abundantly more through you than you could ever imagine.

Are you willing to let go of control and let Him lead? Remember, God can do wonders with a heart that says, "Yes, Lord."

Prayer:

Lord, I come to You as I am, imperfect and flawed. I surrender my will to Yours. Use me for Your glory, and help me trust in Your plan. Strengthen me where I am weak, and guide me to where You want me to be. I am willing, Lord. In Jesus' name, Amen.

Application:

Reflect on areas of your life where you've been striving for perfection instead of surrendering to God's will. Write down one area you will intentionally hand over to Him today.

Contemplation:

- What is God asking me to trust Him with right now?

  _____
  _____
  _____
  _____

- How can I practice saying "yes" to His will today?

  _____
  _____
  _____
  _____

- What is one thing I need to let go of in order to align with His plan?

  _____
  _____
  _____
  _____

DAY 28

Divine Alignment

Opening Scripture:

"Many are the plans in a person's heart, but it is the Lord's purpose that prevails." – Proverbs 19:21 (NIV)

Daily Reflection:

Are you aligned with the Holy Spirit and fully walking in your God-given assignment? It's easy to create plans and pursue our own desires, but true fulfillment comes when we align with God's purpose for our lives. His plans are always greater than ours, and His purpose is eternal.

When you are one with the Holy Spirit, He becomes your guide, your comforter, and your source of truth. Being one with Him means that your decisions, thoughts, and actions flow from a place of communion with God. You're not just pursuing dreams; you're walking in destiny.

Take a moment to evaluate: Are you moving in alignment with God's will, or are you following your own agenda? Surrender your plans to Him and trust in His divine timing.

Prayer:

Lord, thank You for Your purpose in my life. Help me to be one with the Holy Spirit, to hear Your voice clearly, and to walk boldly in the assignment You've placed before me. Align my steps with Your will, and let Your purpose prevail. In Jesus' name, Amen.

Application:

Spend quiet time with God today and ask Him to reveal any areas of your life that may not be aligned with His purpose.

Contemplation:

- What plans in my life might not align with God's purpose?

  _____
  _____
  _____
  _____

- How can I invite the Holy Spirit to guide my decisions daily?

  _____
  _____
  _____
  _____

- What step (s) can I take to walk closer in His will?

  _____
  _____
  _____
  _____

DAY 29

Trust the Blueprint

Opening Scripture:

"For I know the plans I have for you," declares the Lord, *"plans to prosper you and not to harm you, plans to give you hope and a future."* – Jeremiah 29:11 (NIV)

Daily Reflection:

God has a unique blueprint for your life, a divine design that aligns perfectly with His purpose and glory. The only way to uncover that blueprint is to spend intentional time in His presence. It's in the quiet moments of prayer, worship, and reflection that He reveals His plans for you.

You don't have to know every detail to trust in His divine plan. God's vision for your life is greater than anything you could imagine. Trust that He is working behind the scenes, orchestrating every detail for your good and His glory.

Let today be a reminder to pause, seek His guidance, and listen for His voice. When you walk in step with His plan, there is clarity, peace, and purpose.

Prayer:

Lord, I trust You with my life. Reveal the blueprint of Your plans to me as I spend time in Your presence. Help me to surrender my desires and align my heart with Your purpose. Guide me with Your wisdom, and give me the faith to trust Your divine plan. In Jesus' name, Amen.

Application:

Set aside uninterrupted time today to pray, meditate, and journal. Ask God to reveal His purpose for your life.

Contemplation:

- What insights or impressions is God revealing about His plans for my life?

_____
_____
_____
_____

- How can I trust in His timing and plan more fully?

_____
_____
_____
_____

- What steps can I take to align myself with His blueprint?

_____
_____
_____
_____

DAY 30

Strengthen Your Faith

Opening Scripture:

"Above all, taking the shield of faith with which you will be able to quench all the fiery darts of the wicked one." – Ephesians 6:16 (NKJV)

Daily Reflection:

The enemy knows that your faith is the foundation of your relationship with God, which is why he works tirelessly to attack it. He plants seeds of doubt, discouragement, and fear, hoping you will waver. But you are called to stand firm, stronger than the enemy, rooted deeply in God's word and promises.

Faith is not just a feeling; it's a lifestyle. It's an unshakable trust in God's sovereignty, even when circumstances feel overwhelming. Daily prayer, intentional praise, and consistent meditation on Scripture are your tools for spiritual warfare. Live a life that mirrors God's character, walking in love, humility, and obedience.

When your faith is fortified, the enemy has no power over you. Let your life be a testimony of God's strength working through you.

Prayer:

Lord, strengthen my faith so I can withstand the attacks of the enemy. Help me to root myself in Your word and to live a life that reflects Your character. Teach me to trust You fully, pray fervently, and praise You in every situation. I stand firm in Your promises, knowing You are my shield and protector. Amen.

Application:

Begin today by reading Ephesians 6:10–18, focusing on putting on the full armor of God.

Contemplation:

- What area of my life is the enemy trying to attack my faith?

  _____
  _____
  _____
  _____

- What scripture can I reference to speak God's truth over that area in prayer?

  _____
  _____
  _____
  _____

- What specific steps will I take to root myself more deeply in prayer, praise, and Scripture?

  _____
  _____
  _____
  _____

CONGRATULATIONS!

You've reached the end of this devotional—but this is *not* the end of your journey. Every page turned, every prayer whispered, and every reflection journaled has been a seed planted in faith. And in due season, it will bear fruit.

I'm so proud of you for showing up—for God and for yourself. Through the highs and lows, the doubts and discoveries, you've taken meaningful steps toward deeper trust and spiritual growth. That is *Elevaith* — a lifestyle of confident trust in God and the ongoing development of spiritual growth.

Let this devotional remain a trusted companion through every season of your life. Keep it close. Revisit its pages often—you may find that a passage speaks to you differently as you grow. Journal your journey. One day—whether days, months, or even years from now—you'll look back and see how far you've come. That's the beauty of living faith: it expands, deepens, and evolves.

Don't let the journey stop here. Walk boldly in your faith. Let this devotional supplement your commitment to reading the Bible, meditating on God's word, and spending quiet time with Him to share what's on your heart. It is one more tool in your spiritual toolbox. Commit your ways to God, be intentional with your time in the Word, and stay rooted in prayer.

I pray that the peace of God wraps around your heart like a warm embrace, that His wisdom fills your mind, and that His strength empowers every step you take. May you walk boldly in your calling, stay anchored in truth, and overflow with joy—no matter the season. And may you always know that you are seen, known, and deeply loved by your Creator.

"Being confident of this very thing, that He who has begun a good work in you will complete it until the day of Jesus Christ."

—Philippians 1:6 (NKJV)

Whether this is the beginning or somewhere in the middle of your faith walk, know this: it is certainly not the end. It's been an honor to be a part of your journey.

Keep Elevaithing. Keep growing. Keep becoming.

With love,
Elvy McLaurin
Founder & CEO, Elevaith

SCRIPTURE REFERENCES FOR TRUSTING GOD IN TIMES OF UNCERTAINTY

"Trust in the Lord with all your heart, and lean not on your own understanding."

PROVERBS 3:5 (NKJV)

"Commit your way to the Lord, trust also in Him, And He shall bring it to pass."

PSALM 37:5 (NKJV)

"You will keep him in perfect peace, whose mind is stayed on You, because he trusts in You."

ISAIAH 26:3 (NKJV)

"Blessed is the man who trusts in the Lord, and whose hope is the Lord."

JEREMIAH 17:7 (NKJV)

"In God I have put my trust; I will not be afraid. What can man do to me?"

PSALM 56:11 (NKJV)

"The fear of man brings a snare, but whoever trusts in the Lord shall be safe."

PROVERBS 29:25 (NKJV)

"He who trusts in the Lord, mercy shall surround him."

PSALM 32:10(b) (NKJV)

"Whenever I am afraid, I will trust in You."

PSALM 56:3 (NKJV)

SCRIPTURE REFERENCES FOR SPIRITUAL GROWTH AND MATURITY

"But grow in the grace and knowledge of our Lord and Savior Jesus Christ."

2 PETER 3:18(a) (NKJV)

"And do not be conformed to this world, but be transformed by the renewing of your mind..."

ROMANS 12:2(a) (NKJV)

"That Christ may dwell in your hearts through faith; that you, being rooted and grounded in love..."

EPHESIANS 3:17 (NKJV)

"Being confident of this very thing, that He who has begun a good work in you will complete it..."

PHILIPPIANS 1:6 (NKJV)

"Therefore, leaving the discussion of the elementary principles of Christ, let us go on to perfection..."

HEBREWS 6:1(a) (NKJV)

"Examine yourselves as to whether you are in the faith. Test yourselves."

2 CORINTHIANS 13:5(a) (NKJV)

"He must increase, but I must decrease."

JOHN 3:30 (NKJV)

SCRIPTURE REFERENCES FOR GOD'S FAITHFULNESS

"God is not a man, that He should lie, Nor a son of man, that He should repent. Has He said, and will He not do it?"

NUMBERS 23:19(a;b) (NKJV)

"But the Lord is faithful, who will establish you and guard you from the evil one."

2 THESSALONIANS 3:3 (NKJV)

"Through the Lord's mercies we are not consumed, Because His compassions fail not. They are new every morning; Great is Your faithfulness."

LAMENTATIONS 3:22–23 (NKJV)

"Let us hold fast the confession of our hope without wavering, for He who promised is faithful."

HEBREWS 10:23 (NKJV)

"Your faithfulness endures to all generations; You established the earth, and it abides."

PSALM 119:90 (NKJV)

"He who calls you is faithful, who also will do it."

1 THESSALONIANS 5:24 (NKJV)

"If we are faithless, He remains faithful; He cannot deny Himself."

2 TIMOTHY 2:13 (NKJV)

"Therefore know that the Lord your God, He is God, the faithful God"

DEUTERONOMY 7:9 (NKJV)

SCRIPTURE REFERENCES FOR WALKING BY FAITH

"For we walk by faith, not by sight."

2 CORINTHIANS 5:7 (NKJV)

"Now faith is the substance of things hoped for, the evidence of things not seen."

HEBREWS 11:1 (NKJV)

"But without faith it is impossible to please Him..."

HEBREWS 11:6(a) (NKJV)

"Jesus said to him, 'If you can believe, all things are possible to him who believes.'"

MARK 9:23 (NKJV)

"For in it the righteousness of God is revealed from faith to faith..."

ROMANS 1:17(a) (NKJV)

"The just shall live by faith."

GALATIANS 3:11(b) (NKJV)

"And whatever things you ask in prayer, believing, you will receive."

MATTHEW 21:22 (NKJV)

"So then faith comes by hearing, and hearing by the word of God."

ROMANS 10:17 (NKJV)

SCRIPTURE REFERENCES FOR SURRENDER AND OBEDIENCE

"Trust in Him at all times, you people; pour out your heart before Him..."
PSALM 62:8(a,b) (NKJV)

"If you are willing and obedient, you shall eat the good of the land."
ISAIAH 1:19 (NKJV)

"Therefore submit to God. Resist the devil and he will flee from you."
JAMES 4:7 (NKJV)

"Blessed are those who hear the word of God and keep it!"
LUKE 11:28(b) (NKJV)

"Teach me to do Your will, for You are my God..."
PSALM 143:10(a,b) (NKJV)

"If you love Me, keep My commandments."
JOHN 14:15 (NKJV)

"Behold, To obey is better than sacrifice..."
1 SAMUEL 15:22(c) (NKJV)

"Nevertheless, not My will, but Yours, be done."
LUKE 22:42 (NKJV)

SCRIPTURE REFERENCES FOR STRENGTH IN TRIALS

"My brethren, count it all joy when you fall into various trials, 3 knowing that the testing of your faith produces"

JAMES 1:2–3 (NKJV)

"And we know that all things work together for good to those who love God..."

ROMANS 8:28(a) (NKJV)

"The Lord is my strength and my shield; my heart trusted in Him, and I am helped."

PSALM 28:7(a,b) (NKJV)

"When you pass through the waters, I will be with you..."

ISAIAH 43:2(a) (NKJV)

"Many are the afflictions of the righteous, but the Lord delivers him out of them all."

PSALM 34:19 (NKJV)

"In the world you will have tribulation; but be of good cheer, I have overcome the world."

JOHN 16:33(b) (NKJV)

"Cast your burden on the Lord, and He shall sustain you..."

PSALM 55:22(a,b) (NKJV)

"Though I walk in the midst of trouble, You will revive me..."

PSALM 138:7(a) (NKJV)

ABOUT THE AUTHOR

Now that we've journeyed together to *Elevaith* your life in God through Jesus Christ, I want to share a piece of my own journey.

I'm Elvy McLaurin—a devoted mother to three beautiful daughters, Zion, Zania, and Zelani, whom I raise with deep faith and intention. I'm also a Certified Life Coach specializing in Spiritual Wellness, a speaker, an author, and above all, a woman after God's heart. But before the titles and accomplishments came the trials, the pain, and the refining process that shaped the woman I am today.

I was born and raised in New Orleans, Louisiana. I'm the second oldest of five children. At just 11 years old, I lost my mother—a loss that introduced me to grief before I could fully understand life. Only a few years later, Hurricane Katrina hit. Like many, my family was displaced and left to navigate uncertainty, confusion, and emotional upheaval. These events left imprints that I would carry with me for years, but they also planted seeds of resilience.

After my mother's passing, my grandmother Jo Ann McLaurin stepped in to raise us. I owe so much to her. Her love and sacrifice became the steady ground beneath our feet. Though I didn't fully realize it then, God was already writing a story through my pain.

As I grew older, I discovered my gift for encouraging others. What started as sharing scripture-based devotionals, heartfelt prayers, and uplifting thoughts with my close circle gradually evolved into something greater. Recognizing a broader need for spiritual encouragement, I felt called to extend my ministry beyond my immediate community. My passion for fulfilling God's purpose and being a blessing to others led to the birth of this book. I felt compelled to pour into others the same way others have poured into me. I've always had a passion for inspiring people through biblical truth and authentic connection. My life experiences only made that call clearer.

In 2013, I became a mother. The love I felt was overwhelming in the best way. I welcomed a second daughter in 2015, got married in 2017 and gave birth to my youngest daughter in 2021. But behind the scenes, my life was unraveling. Just months after giving birth, I was also diagnosed with major postpartum depression. In 2022, my husband and I separated. That season was one of the most challenging times of my life.

Suddenly, I found myself navigating single motherhood—raising three children on my own after building a home I thought would last. My kids and I lived in a hotel for some time before moving into an apartment. I felt broken, lost, and spiritually depleted. But even in the pain, God was near.

That season forced me to re-learn everything—how to be a mother, how to stand on my own, and most importantly, how to fully rely on God. I started over—not just in life, but in my walk with Him. I prayed, meditated, and studied the Word with more intention than ever before. In doing so, I discovered who I was in Christ, and that changed everything.

My relationship with God became my lifeline. He gave me peace that didn't make sense and strength I didn't know I had. He surrounded me with what I call "destiny helpers"—people who supported, prayed for, and encouraged me. I'm forever grateful for them.

In 2023, I became a Certified Life Coach specializing in Spiritual Wellness. It was through that journey I began to understand my purpose on a deeper level. I hadn't gone through all that pain for nothing—something beautiful was being birthed from the ashes. As Isaiah 61:3(b) (NKJV) says, *"To give them beauty for ashes, the oil of joy for mourning, the garment of praise for the spirit of heaviness."* I now walk boldly in the healing, strength, and identity God has given me.

Today, at 33, I see how every part of my story—every heartache, every breakthrough—is connected to His divine plan. My journey has become a testimony of God's grace, favor, and redemptive power. Along the way, I've built an even deeper bond with my daughters—they're my "mini besties."

This devotional, and everything I share, flows from a place of deep conviction: that with God, nothing is ever wasted. My journey is rooted in unwavering faith and anchored by three guiding pillars—prayer, patience, and perseverance.

I pray that my journey, wisdom, and faith inspire you to embrace your purpose, overcome challenges, and draw closer to God.

With love,
Elvy McLaurin

Connect with Elevaith

EMAIL: Elevaith@gmail.com
PHONE: (504) 358 - 8650
WEBSITE: https://linktr.ee/elevaithlife
INSTAGRAM: elevaithbyelvy
FACEBOOK: Elevaith Life Coaching
X: ElevaithbyElvy

Services Offered:

Faith Based Life Coaching
Speaker
Author
Executive Training
Workshop Facilitator

www.ingramcontent.com/pod-product-compliance
Lightning Source LLC
Chambersburg PA
CBHW060501090426
42735CB00011B/2068